TITANS
OF BUSINESS

JAY-Z

Richard Spilsbury

Chicago, Illinois

www.capstonepub.com
Visit our website to find out more information about Heinemann-Raintree books.

To order:
☎ Phone 800-747-4992
💻 Visit www.capstonepub.com to browse our catalog and order online.

Edited by Mark Friedman, Nancy Dickmann, and Claire Throp
Designed by Richard Parker
Picture research by Liz Alexander
Original Illustrations © Capstone Global Library Ltd 2013
Illustrations by Darren Lingard
Originated by Capstone Global Library Ltd
Printed and bound in China by CTPS

16 15 14 13 12
10 9 8 7 6 5 4 3 2 1

Library of Congress Cataloging-in-Publication Data
Spilsbury, Richard, 1963-
 Jay-Z / Richard Spilsbury.—1st ed.
   p. cm.—(Titans of business)
 Includes bibliographical references and index.
 ISBN 978-1-4329-6430-6 (hb)—ISBN 978-1-4329-6437-5 (pb) 1. Jay-Z, 1969—Juvenile literature. 2. Rap musicians—United States—Biography—Juvenile literature. 3. Success in business—Juvenile literature. I. Title.
 ML3930.J38S65 2013
 782.421649092—dc23   2011050758
 [B]

Acknowledgments
We would like to thank the following for permission to reproduce photographs: Alamy p. 11 (© David Hoffman Photo Library); Corbis pp. 9 (© John Van Hasselt/Sygma), 16 (© Mitchell Gerber), 17 (© Nicolas Six/Danser), 18 (© Larry Ford), 27 (© Sayre Berman), 35 (© Gary Cameron/X00044/Reuters), 39 (© Andrew Goetz), 41 (© Sara De Boer/Retna Ltd); Getty Images p. 36; Getty Images pp. 5 (Ethan Miller/WireImage), 7 (Michael Ochs Archives), 8 (Al Pereira/Michael Ochs Archives), 13 (Anthony Barboza), 15 (Al Pereira/Michael Ochs Archives), 19 (Michael Ochs Archives), 20 (Chris Walter/WireImage), 22 (Adam Rountree), 23 (Scott Gries), 25 (Todd Plitt), 29 (Shawn Ehlers/WireImage), 30 (Dimitrios Kambouris), 31 (Gustavo Caballero/WireImage), 33 (Charley Gallay/Getty Images for Gucci), 37 (William Thomas Cain/Bloomberg), 43 (Astrid Stawiarz); Press Association Images pp. 21 (Mary Altaffer/AP), 24 (Kevork Djansezian/AP), 32 (Kathy Willens/AP).

Cover photograph reproduced with permission of Rex Features/Huw John (main image) and Shutterstock/© Eky Studio (background image).

Every effort has been made to contact copyright holders of any material reproduced in this book. Any omissions will be rectified in subsequent printings if notice is given to the publisher.

Disclaimer
All the Internet addresses (URLs) given in this book were valid at the time of going to press. However, due to the dynamic nature of the Internet, some addresses may have changed, or sites may have changed or ceased to exist since publication. While the author and publisher regret any inconvenience this may cause readers, no responsibility for any such changes can be accepted by either the author or the publisher.

Contents

Find out what you need to do to have a successful career like Jay-Z.

Read what Jay-Z has said or what has been said about him.

Learn more about the people who influenced Jay-Z.

Discover more about businesses that have been important during Jay-Z's career.

Words printed in **bold** are explained in the glossary.

Introducing Jay-Z

Jay-Z was born in one of the poorest areas of New York City, and he became one of the richest people in the United States. His musical skills have produced more number one albums than anyone but the Beatles. His live shows can sell out in a few minutes. Jay-Z's business skills have helped him set up and run successful record companies, a fashion brand, and other **ventures**.

Jay-Z's music

Jay-Z is a star of **hip-hop** music. He has been a rapper or **MC** (master of ceremonies) since his teenage years. The **lyrics** and raps he creates are about his own experiences—from selling drugs in a poor community, to living in luxury.

When Jay-Z was starting out, hip-hop was only heard on the streets of U.S. cities, but now it's one of the biggest-selling pop styles. A major reason for this is Jay-Z's ability to make hip-hop appeal to a wider audience.

How did Jay-Z become a titan of business? What risks and choices did he take and make along the way? Could we learn from his story so that we might succeed in business, too?

Entrepreneur

Jay-Z is hip-hop's greatest **entrepreneur**. He has consistently spotted new opportunities to make money from his music and set up and run his own businesses to do so. Like all entrepreneurs, he has risked losing everything if he fails, but Jay-Z's skills have made sure that most of his ventures have succeeded.

> "This is a journey for a kid from Brooklyn to play the biggest stage in the world."
>
> Jay-Z

Jay-Z plays at the biggest concert venue in Las Vegas, Nevada, on New Year's Eve 2010. He had already been one of the most mesmerizing live hip-hop performers for more than a decade.

The Young Shawn Carter

Jay-Z's real name is Shawn Corey Carter. He was born in Brooklyn in New York City on December 4, 1969. Shawn's early experiences growing up in a poor neighborhood had a big impact on his life in music and business.

Carter family life

Shawn was the fourth child of Gloria Carter and Adnis Reeves. He has two sisters, Michelle and Andrea, and a brother, Eric. His parents struggled to pay the bills. Gloria worked as a clerk in an insurance company, and Adnis only found occasional work.

When Shawn was five years old, the family moved from one part of Brooklyn into Marcy Houses in the Bedford-Stuyvesant neighborhood because rent was cheaper. The apartments in the Marcy **housing project** were small and cramped, and the area was poor and run down.

Musical beginnings

Music was an important part of Shawn's life from the beginning. Gloria and Adnis were huge music fans, and each had their own prized record collections. Shawn was a shy boy, but he loved the music that filled their home. He liked to drum on the kitchen table and make up rhymes to the music. He often wrote rhymes for hours at a time. Later he learned to memorize lines so he did not have to carry around paper in his pocket.

"My mom and pop had an extensive record collection, so Michael Jackson and Stevie Wonder and all of those sounds and souls of **Motown** filled the house."

Jay-Z

Stevie Wonder was a major star, and a source of inspiration for Jay-Z when he was younger.

Troubled time

In 1980, Shawn's father walked out on his family. This was devastating for Gloria and the children. Gloria took on several jobs to earn enough money to make a living, but she was not around as much to control her children.

Shawn had been a good student at school, but as life got more difficult at home he started to get into more and more trouble. He skipped school and spent more time on the streets. Life was tough on the streets—young people were stealing, there were constant fights and violence, and many people had guns.

Jay-Z with his friend and hip-hop **mentor** Jaz-O. Jaz-O helped to teach Jay-Z about the music industry and how to make commercially successful hip-hop tracks.

The upside of the poor, cramped housing where many African Americans lived in New York was that close communities formed there. The downside was that problems caused by poverty, including crime and drugs, spread fast.

Troubled place

Many residents of Marcy Houses were out of work and poorly educated. They struggled to improve their lives. Some were using drugs to escape the hopelessness. In the mid-1980s, the most widely used drug there was **crack cocaine**, because it was cheap and had strong effects.

Crack cocaine was also very **addictive**. Drug addicts became desperate to pay for their next "fix." They usually stole, and were often violent. This meant that Marcy residents lived in fear of crime and their loved ones becoming addicted, too.

The shooting

Drugs were even part of Shawn's home life because his brother Eric was a crack addict. Like most users, Eric stole to pay for his drugs—either from shops, people on the street, or family. When Shawn was 12 years old, Eric stole Shawn's ring. Shawn was so angry that he borrowed a gun from a man he knew and shot his brother in the shoulder.

Eric wasn't badly wounded, but he had to go to the hospital. Shawn was terrified that he'd end up in prison, but Eric didn't involve the police. Jay-Z has since said that this terrible event was the one thing in his life that he regrets.

Hustling

At first, the only way Shawn could see to make money for himself and his family was to become a **hustler** (someone who aggressively sells something). Most people he knew were either taking drugs, selling them, or both. So Shawn started hustling drugs when he was 13 but avoided crack, partly because he saw how that drug was messing up Eric.

In spite of his mother's protests, Shawn left school to start hustling full time. He was good at it and made lots of money, but it was a dangerous and violent lifestyle. He was shot at three times by rival hustlers in his teenage years.

"Back then I would say it was like two things. Like, it was either you was doing it [drugs] or you was moving [selling] it."
Jay-Z talking about drugs

Crack addicts inhale vapor released by heating
the drug for a sudden and short-lived high. The
addicted created wealth for hustlers such as Shawn,
but many spiraled into poor health and crime.

Starting Out in Music

Shawn was getting into hustling, but in the background there was always music. Shawn was growing up at the dawn of the hip-hop age.

There was great excitement about hip-hop in Shawn's neighborhood. This style of music had begun in New York City, where rappers such as Grandmaster Flash performed in city clubs. Hip-hop records were on the charts, and local artists such as the Sugarhill Gang had become big stars among young African Americans. The music often described the city life they knew. Shawn and his friends dreamed of becoming rappers and getting rich through music.

Musical skills

At home, Shawn spent hours on end in front of a mirror practicing his rapping skills and perfecting his **flow**. In hip-hop, this means keeping a long stream of lyrics going smoothly and rhythmically. He'd think of new lines while he was out on the streets and write them down in a green notebook that he always kept safe at home. He memorized the lines and showed them off at rap competitions in the school cafeteria. This was when friends, including rising rapper Chris Wallace (also known as Biggie Smalls), first started to respect Shawn's musical skills.

Sugarhill Gang

The Sugarhill Gang is a U.S. hip-hop group. In 1979, they released "Rapper's Delight." It was the first rap hit record and reached the U.S. Top 40. The record was the first on Sugar Hill Records, a hip-hop **record company** named after an area of New York City that was famous for music in the early 20th century.

The Sugarhill Gang, seen here in 1980, led the way for hip-hop stars.

Shawn becomes Jay-Z

Shawn left school in the late 1980s. He continued to practice rap along with neighborhood rappers and friends. In 1988, he recorded a tape of his vocals with rappers Big Daddy Kane and Jaz-O. It was played in the neighborhood, and his smooth-flowing rap style was noticed and appreciated for the first time by the public. Many rappers had stage names. Shawn chose the name Jay-Z. This was partly because he worked closely with the similarly named Jaz-O, and also because the J and Z **subway** trains had stops in Brooklyn.

Learning about the music industry

Entrepreneurs are not born knowing everything about their businesses. They often have to learn from others. Jay-Z first learned about how the music industry works through Jaz-O.

Jaz-O signed a **recording contract** with the EMI record company. This is an agreement to make an artist's records. Record companies **promote** or advertise music artists, for example, by organizing concerts, getting radio stations to play their music, and **distributing** their records to music stores to sell. Jay-Z took part in his friend's concerts and appeared on Jaz-O's records, and in the process he learned how the music business worked.

"I was taught in my family to believe that anything worth having you had to work extremely hard for. But rap came easy for me. I wouldn't say I took it for granted, but I didn't realize I had a gift until I made that tape."

Jay-Z speaking about the 1988 tape

Jay-Z started out knowing little about the business side of music, but he soon learned.

The right people

Jay-Z's ability to find people who could help him is one of the keys to his success. In 1992, he met music manager Damon Dash.

Dash's job was to find new artists and fix them up with a recording contract. He and Jay-Z hit it off immediately, perhaps because they recognized the same drive to succeed in each other. Dash became Jay-Z's manager. He paid for Jay-Z to record tracks for an album called *Reasonable Doubt*, featuring some of Jay-Z's talented friends, such as Biggie Smalls.

Jay-Z realized that his music and style could appeal to and make money from a larger audience, and that Damon Dash was the man to help him make it happen.

"We knew we had something the people wanted, so instead of quitting we built it ourselves."

Jay-Z

Do it yourself

Dash tried to persuade record companies to take on Jay-Z and his album, but failed. So he and Jay-Z made copies of a single from the album, called "In My Lifetime," and started selling them from the trunk of a car. By playing it out loud in the streets on a **stereo**, they got local people interested. Word got around about the single, and a New York City record company called Payday Records agreed to distribute it in 1995.

Jay-Z did not imagine when he started his hip-hop career that the music and its style would become global. These are Korean performers at hip-hop's Battle of the Year in 2004.

Damon Dash

Damon Dash was born in Harlem, New York City, in 1971. He first made money by renting clubs and charging people to come to parties there. As a musical manager, he promoted his acts through **rap battles** in which rappers competed against each other. He was so rich that he once devoted a whole story of his house to clothes!

Roc-A-Fella

Payday Records failed to get "In My Lifetime" widely known, and Jay-Z fell out with the company. This was a turning point in Jay-Z's life. Most artists would have been desperate to keep a contract with any record company, but Jay-Z decided to set up his own record label to take control of his business.

In 1996, Jay-Z and Dash started up their own record company—Roc-A-Fella. They finally released *Reasonable Doubt*, which sold well for a **debut** album. More importantly, it was a big hit with music critics, who loved its mix of personal storytelling and clever rhyming.

Damon Dash (left), Jay-Z, and Kareem Burke (right) in the offices at Roc-A-Fella Records. Burke was an investor and cofounder of the new company, but he had little creative involvement.

Making more money

In order to distribute the album, Roc-A-Fella signed a deal with a larger record company called Priority Records. In return, Priority took a large share of **profits** from each record sold.

However, Jay-Z, his album, and Roc-A-Fella were becoming well known in the music business. The team had not profited from the sales of *Reasonable Doubt* as much as they would have liked. In 1997, Jay-Z approached the major hip-hop record company Def Jam. They agreed to sign a deal to make and promote Roc-A-Fella's records—and share the profits evenly.

Run-DMC was one of the most popular hip-hop acts of the 1980s. They were the first rap superstars, and their unique music and clothing proved to be a major influence on hip-hop culture.

Def Jam

Def Jam was founded in 1984 by Russell Simmons and Rick Rubin. Simmons was a drug dealer and hip-hop **producer**, and Rubin was a student with a good ear for new musical talent. Def Jam produced many of the best-known rap acts of the 1980s, 1990s, and 2000s, from Run-DMC to Public Enemy.

Musical Superstar

Jay-Z's real turnaround came when he started to appeal to a wider audience. By selling hip-hop to large numbers of white people (not just African American teenagers), Jay-Z could make more money.

In 1997, Jay-Z released his next album, *In My Lifetime, Vol. 1*. The lyrics were less violent than before, and at times the music had more of a pop sound. This made it more appealing to a wider audience.

One reason for the change in language was the recent death of his great friend Biggie Smalls. Smalls and another rapper, Tupac Shakur, were both murdered as a result of growing conflict between rappers from different parts of the country. Insults and threats of violence in their lyrics led to real-life attacks.

The Notorious B.I.G., formerly known as Biggie Smalls, rapping in 1995. He was the top-selling solo male act in the United States that year. His death in 1997 had a big impact on the direction of hip-hop.

Hard Knock Life

Jay-Z's big breakthrough came in 1998 with *Vol. 2... Hard Knock Life*. Its title song used the chorus from the Broadway musical *Annie* to tell the tale of a rapper's rise to fame. Jay-Z had cleverly mixed a mainstream pop song with hip-hop to come up with a hit. The album sold five million copies and earned him a **Grammy** award.

Jay-Z refused to go to the Grammy ceremony as a protest against how few awards rappers were given. This was a clever business move. It made him look tough again at a time when music critics and hip-hop fans thought he was trying too hard to be popular.

Combining his rapping and themes from the popular musical *Annie* helped Jay-Z become a hip-hop superstar.

"The overall strategy [plan] is to increase [Jay-Z's] visibility and make him that **crossover** artist without sacrificing his full street credibility."

Jazz Young, Def Jam

Shock

In 2003, Jay-Z shocked his fans and the whole hip-hop world. He announced that his forthcoming *Black Album* would be his last because he needed a break. Few people could understand why he would retire as a recording artist at the peak of his success. After all, from 1999 to 2003, Jay-Z's five albums had all been successful on the U.S. hip-hop charts. But retiring proved to be a good business decision because it attracted public interest in Jay-Z and helped make the album a best seller.

Jay-Z held a press conference to announce the release of his *Black Album* in 2003.

Russell Simmons, cofounder of Def Jam, with the new CEO of the company, Jay-Z, at a press conference. This was one of the most important positions in the hip-hop recording industry.

New direction

But at the start of 2005, there was another, bigger surprise. Jay-Z became **Chief Executive Officer (CEO)** at Def Jam Records. This role gave him day-to-day control over producing records, spotting new talent, and promoting the company's artists. It was completely unheard of for an artist to have such control in a big record company.

However, Jay-Z had proven to be both a successful artist and a highly successful businessman at Roc-A-Fella. He had the business skills to ensure further hits for Def Jam and help it grow even bigger. Jay-Z has said that he realized the importance of taking the job because African American **executives** were rare in the music industry.

Change for success

Jay-Z has always been good at making changes to ensure his businesses are more successful. For example, at Def Jam he spent time with employees to hear their ideas for improving the business and started to reward staff who were **innovative**. These changes helped Def Jam become more successful than ever.

The artist returns

Jay-Z had taken control of his musical career through business deals with Def Jam. As the company's CEO, he was now calling the shots—and had the satisfaction of discovering stars such as Rihanna. But he still missed making his own music.

At the end of 2006, Jay-Z came out of musical retirement with the release of his comeback album *Kingdom Come*. It was successful, but some Def Jam artists said the CEO was concentrating more on promoting his own work than theirs. At the end of 2007, Jay-Z realized that he could not balance making his own music with his CEO role at Def Jam. He resigned.

Jay-Z looks on proudly as Rihanna, one of the stars he discovered at Def Jam, wins an award.

"In our industry, they want to be like Jay. And not just because he's the best lyricist, but because he's taken control of his career... If Jay-Z says your stage show isn't hot, it's not hot."

DJ Semtex, Def Jam manager

Changes in the industry

However, there was another reason why Jay-Z left Def Jam. His earnings at the company were directly related to sales, and the public was buying fewer albums. For example, his 2007 album *American Gangster* sold only a third of the (three million) total of his 2003 album *Black Album 3*, even though he was more famous globally.

The major reason for this was that by the late 2000s more people were getting music without paying for it, either through illegal **downloads** from websites or by making their own copies of CDs. This hurt the sales of all artists and record companies, not just Jay-Z and Def Jam.

Jay-Z returned to the studio in 2006 but struggled to balance the Def Jam CEO role with his creative output.

Going live

In the late 2000s, Jay-Z did promotional tours for Def Jam, including headlining at Glastonbury Festival in England in 2008. But still, his earnings were tied in with record sales rather than the popularity of the shows. In 2008, Jay-Z left Def Jam Records and signed a deal with Live Nation.

Live Nation was a new kind of business. It combined the roles of a record company (signing and promoting artists) with a concert company, which specializes in live shows and **merchandising**. The company actually owned many of the concert halls where its artists appeared, and therefore took in more money from the ticket sales.

Roc Nation

Live Nation struck a deal with Jay-Z: that he would go on concert tours, make records, give **copyright** of his music to Live Nation, and set up a record label called Roc Nation. The deal guaranteed him an enormous $150 million income over 10 years.

Roc Nation is a record label and artist management business that Jay-Z uses to sign up new talent and produce his own material. His first album on Roc Nation was *The Blueprint 3* in 2009. It won three Grammy awards and produced the globally successful single "Empire State of Mind," featuring Alicia Keys.

"In meeting with superstars about potential deals, there are some who spit out 'How much can I get?...' When we sat down with Jay-Z, 'How much money are you going to pay me?' came up in maybe the seventh conversation. The first conversation was, 'Can we change the business together?'"

Michael Rapino, President of Live Nation

Signing with Live Nation was good business because it guaranteed Jay-Z high earnings regardless of how well his records sold!

Business Empire

Jay-Z's first successes came with music, but he soon began to expand his empire into other areas of business, from clothing to hotels.

Jay-Z got the idea for another business venture from watching his fans. Jay-Z noticed that many of his fans wore clothes from the same company he did, which he often mentioned in his lyrics. In the early 1990s, he approached that particular clothing label about an **endorsement** deal.

Endorsement is when a company pays someone famous to promote their products, for example, by wearing or using them on stage or in public, or advertising them on television. The clothing company refused to make a promotion deal with Jay-Z and Damon Dash. So, they decided not to bother to endorse other people's products and to start their own clothing label instead.

"The clothes are an extension of me. The music is an extension of me. All my businesses are part of the culture, so I have to stay true to whatever I'm feeling at the time, whatever direction I'm heading in. And hopefully, everyone follows."

Jay-Z

Rocawear

In 1999, Jay-Z and Damon Dash launched their clothing company, Rocawear. Instead of rapping about other people's products, Jay-Z could now rap about his own! Rocawear used the success of hip-hop music to sell clothes linked to hip-hop culture.

Jay-Z introduced a mobile clothes store, the "Roc Pop Shop," to accompany him to concerts and events. When Jay-Z toured or performed with other rappers, they wore Rocawear clothing, too. It grew into such a success that Jay-Z eventually sold the Rocawear clothing company for $204 million in 2007.

Jay-Z shows off his Rocawear clothing line at the grand opening of his mobile clothes store, Roc Pop Shop, in 2006.

Designing and selling sneakers

Jay-Z expanded into footwear, too. He met advertising executive Steve Stoute, who was trying to relaunch Reebok sports clothing, which had become unfashionable. Jay-Z was soon helping to redesign footwear for Reebok and was seen rapping with 50 Cent wearing S. Carter collection sneakers. They became the fastest-selling shoes in Reebok's history. Stoute's instinct was right. The link with Jay-Z helped to make Reebok products cool and fashionable. It rescued the company by reconnecting it with young, urban culture.

Steve Stoute

Steve Stoute (left of picture) grew up in New York City and worked in the music business until 2000, where he learned a lot about endorsements. As an advertising executive, he specializes in celebrity endorsements. He says that he developed his insight into **consumer** behavior by watching the way people shop.

Spreading influence

In 2008, Jay-Z expanded his business empire in yet another new direction when he set up the New York City-based Translation Advertising **agency** with Steve Stoute. The idea of the agency is to boost a company's image by linking them up with cool hip-hop stars, such as Jay-Z. This helps the companies sell their products—not just to white audiences, but also to African American, Asian, and **Hispanic** people who like hip-hop.

For example, the Translation Advertising agency organized a link up between the chewing gum company Wrigley and rapper Chris Brown. Brown's song "Forever" featured a jingle from an old Wrigley's advertisement. This helped the company boost sales of its gum.

Sales of products can increase when linked with well-known artists such as Chris Brown.

Other kinds of entertainment

Jay-Z also branched out into other areas of entertainment. He invested in a chain of nightclubs called 40/40, and in a New York City restaurant. In 2004, he became co-owner of his favorite basketball team, the New Jersey Nets. His fame gets the team widespread publicity, and has helped them attract new players and funding for a new stadium in Jay-Z's home borough of Brooklyn.

Jay-Z has also been involved in film and theater. Some of his films are of concerts or compilations of his music videos, but he also starred alongside Damon Dash as a gangster in the 2002 feature film *State Property*. In 2009, he invested in a new Broadway musical called *Fela!*, about a famous African musician. It was a big hit.

Jay-Z with his own Nets jersey. In the 2012–2013 season, the team will become the Brooklyn Nets, when they move to their new stadium. This was one of Jay-Z's requests when investing in the team.

Jay-Z had his first megahit with "Hard Knock Life (Ghetto Anthem)," based on a song from *Annie*. In 2011, he started work on a film of the same musical with Will Smith.

Film producer

In 2011, Jay-Z moved into film production. A film producer is responsible for overseeing a film project from beginning to end—from finding funds and choosing scripts and stars, to making sure everybody knows about it. As a first project, Jay-Z is planning a remake of the musical *Annie* with his friend and business partner, actor-director Will Smith. The story of a white girl who escapes from an orphanage in the 1930s seems a curious choice for a rapper, but it's mainly about someone making a better life for herself. Jay-Z knows that's a story that sells. In the film, the role of Annie will be played by Will Smith's daughter, Willow.

"When the TV version [of *Annie*] came on, I was drawn to it. It was the struggle of this poor kid in this environment and how her life changed... It immediately **resonated**."

Jay-Z

Unsuccessful projects

Not all of Jay-Z's new ventures were successful. In 2005, Jay-Z worked with the car company Chrysler Motors to develop a new line of cars. Jay-Z jeeps had huge chrome wheels, cream-colored leather interiors, and a digital stereo preloaded with all of his music! However, it was thought that Chrysler Motors became concerned about Jay-Z's criminal past and scrapped the deal.

In 2007, another car company, General Motors, unveiled a new color for a range of their cars. It was called Jay-Z blue, and Jay-Z had created it for them.

In 2007, Jay-Z tried to expand into the hotel business. He bought land in an expensive area of New York City, where he planned to build a luxury hotel called The J Hotel. However, construction was halted in 2008 due to lack of funds caused by the **global economic crisis**. When his 40/40 nightclub in Las Vegas failed after just eight months, Jay-Z was forced to sell it. However, he kept the name so that he could open more nightclubs in other parts of the world, such as London and Tokyo. The year wasn't a total failure, however—it was in 2008 that Jay-Z married fellow superstar, Beyoncé.

Exploit success

All entrepreneurs experience failure. The trick is to learn from your failures and be ready to exploit success. That means you use the fame, experience, and contacts you made by being successful in one industry to succeed in others. For example, Jay-Z exploited his success in music to set up businesses in advertising, film, and other industries.

Jay-Z at the unveiling of the 2007 GMC Yukon Denali painted in his Jay-Z Blue color.

The Jay-Z Brand

A **brand** is the name of a company's product (or group of products) that is often represented by a slogan or **logo**, such as Apple and their apple symbol. Once a brand is well known for its positive features, such as good design or reliability, people are more likely to buy that brand of products. Sometimes a brand can be a person, too. Jay-Z has made himself into one of the biggest brands in the music world.

Building a personal brand means building up a reputation so that people know what you stand for. When your name means something to people, you can start using it to sell products or services. Jay-Z presents himself as a straight-talking and honest, self-made man. People like the fact that he pulled himself up from a life of poverty and crime to become a successful businessman. Because people like the Jay-Z brand, they buy what he sells.

Jay-Z has expensive taste in cars. As a successful businessman, he can afford to buy the car he wants.

Promoting the brand

A brand is only useful as long as it's famous. Jay-Z constantly advertises his name, his music, and the products linked to him. For example, when the Nets play basketball, his music blasts out during the game. The team tour bus features a picture of the sneakers he designed on the side of it—and when the team wins, they always celebrate at the 40/40 nightclub owned by Jay-Z!

A lot of people think Jay-Z is cool. When a company like Reebok pays him to help design and advertise their shoes, they hope their products will seem cool, too.

"He understands himself as a brand, and it's incredibly well thought out... He's very consistent, and he won't settle. If something's not right, he's not going to do it for more money. He'll wait to get it right. He has a wonderful taste level about where he wants to take the brand...and himself."

Neil Cole, Iconix Brand Group, which bought Rocawear

Critics of the brand

An important part of Jay-Z's brand is the way he has never forgotten who or what he was in the past. But some critics have accused Jay-Z of **exaggerating** stories about his past to make the Jay-Z brand more interesting.

Klein, a famous Brooklyn drug dealer who is mentioned in Jay-Z's lyrics, has claimed that Jay-Z lies about his past and really didn't sell many drugs at all. Jay-Z stands by his version of events, but we may never know the truth.

> "In the 80s Jay was not trying to be a drug dealer, he was trying to be a rapper. In order for him to transcend [go beyond the limits of] himself into this hell of a dude, he had to take characters of guys from the 80s; one being myself."
>
> Klein

Other critics say that Jay-Z is more interested in making money than writing songs that really make people think. They say that he has not produced groundbreaking music since the *Black Album* in 2003. Nas, a fellow hip-hop artist, has attacked the music industry's control over hip-hop and also Jay-Z for going along with it. But Jay-Z believes that hip-hop music is about gaining wealth and being a success. Hip-hop fans are happy to see their heroes succeed and want to be like them.

In 2010, the rapper M.I.A., a recent star of hip-hop, said that Jay-Z may have sold out by wanting to become a household name all over the planet. She hoped that artists such as Nas could still be heard by the public even though their music might be less easy to connect with.

The Future for Jay-Z

Jay-Z has won 10 Grammy awards and sold 45 million albums over the years, and he remains influential and successful in the hip-hop world. Other artists and businesses are desperate for his endorsements to improve their public image. He continues to create new music and tour the world.

Jay-Z is part of popular music's most high-profile couple through his marriage to Beyoncé Knowles, superstar R&B singer. But in 2003, when he first retired from music, Jay-Z said rap is a young man's game that has to come to an end one day. Now that he is in his 40s, how much longer will he want to be involved in the business?

Continued success

Jay-Z realized he could be so much more successful if he broke away from being just a rapper and also became a businessman. Through careful control of his music and other businesses, Jay-Z has built a personal fortune of around $450 million. He earns a fortune from his nonmusic businesses. For example, he continues to get a cut of the profits from Rocawear's annual $700 million in sales because he still helps design the clothing.

His new business ventures include producing a new animated series, making the new *Annie* film, and opening a new restaurant in London that donates some of its profits to charity each month. As long as he is involved enough in hip-hop to keep his public profile high, he should guarantee his future in business.

> "It's all about what's next, and that's what drives me after all this time."
>
> Jay-Z

Beyoncé and Jay-Z's first baby was born in 2012, so Jay-Z now has to juggle parenthood with remaining successful in music and business.

How to Become an Entrepreneur

Jay-Z's musical talent, ambition, and drive propelled him from Marcy to megastardom! What makes successful entrepreneurs, and what can we learn from Jay-Z's career?

Spot opportunities

A successful entrepreneur is someone who can spot a business opportunity. Jay-Z moved from Def Jam to Live Nation because it increased his income regardless of record sales.

Keep trying

There's a famous saying: "Success is one percent inspiration and 99 percent perspiration." To be successful, you have to work hard. Jay-Z's hard work and dedication paid off, but it didn't happen overnight. He didn't have his first big hit until he was in his 30s.

Ask for advice

It's vital to take advice from others on how to get started and what it takes to succeed. Jay-Z learned from the help he received. For example, Steve Stoute showed him how to make money by letting other businesses use his hip-hop brand.

Take risks

Entrepreneurs take risks to find out if their ideas will succeed. Jay-Z's career has been all about risk-taking, and one of the biggest risks was forming Roc-A-Fella. If it had failed, he could have damaged his reputation, as well as his bank balance!

Communicate!

Jay-Z can communicate the story of his life to a wide audience using his rapping skills. He can also communicate effectively to businesses to get himself excellent deals. Top entrepreneurs are always excellent communicators who can help other people appreciate their ideas or skills.

> "I've never looked at myself and said that I need to be a certain way to be around a certain sort of people... I've always wanted to stay true to myself, and I've managed to do that."
>
> Jay-Z

In business, Jay-Z always aims to keep creative control. His brand tie-ins are rarely one-offs, and they link to his work rather than just his name.

Glossary

addictive something that people are unable to stop doing or using, such as smoking cigarettes or crack cocaine

agency business providing a particular service for other businesses, such as advertising their products

brand logo, name, and features of a business that make people recognize it

Chief Executive Officer (CEO) highest-ranking person in a company; the boss

consumer person who buys goods or uses services

copyright legal ownership of music or other artistic product. Other people ask permission and/or pay the copyright holder to use the product.

crack cocaine type of powerful drug in the form of small crystals that is cheap to make and highly addictive

crossover result of changing from one style of music to another

debut first appearance of a performer

distribute send goods such as CDs to stores so that large numbers of people can buy them

download move data or files of words, images, music, programs, or videos from one computer to another

endorsement public action or statement that shows someone famous liking or using a particular product

entrepreneur person who takes financial risks to set up and run new businesses

exaggerate boast or make something seem better or worse than it actually is

executive someone who has a senior or important job within a company

flow in rap, the smooth stringing together of many words into rhythmic phrases that fit in with the background music

global economic crisis period from 2008 and beyond when banks lost money. This had a great impact on countries worldwide when businesses failed, jobs were lost, and people had to sell their homes.

Grammy name of an outstanding achievement award for musicians from the U.S. National Academy of Recording Arts

hip-hop type of modern dance music mixing spoken words and a steady beat, often including samples from other people's music

Hispanic   person whose first language is Spanish, and who is from Spain or another Spanish-speaking country, such as Mexico

housing project   blocks of cheap houses or apartments built by governments for poor families

hustler   person who aggressively sells something, often illegally

innovative   new way of doing or making something

logo   symbol or image that a company uses as its special sign

lyrics   words to a song

MC   stands for master of ceremonies, often used to describe a rapper in hip-hop music

mentor   person with experience in an industry or subject who helps and advises someone with less experience

merchandising   products connected with a particular film, television series, person, or event, such as Jay-Z posters or T-shirts

Motown   famous record label and style of R&B music, especially during the 1960s and 1970s

producer   person who manages a recording, television, or film project. A music producer finds a singer or band, finds a song for them to record, and promotes them and their product.

profit   financial gain made from a business or investment

promote   help sell a product or make someone or something more popular

rap battle   live competition where rappers try to outdo each other in performance

record company   company that finds singers or bands and songs, then records, advertises, and sells their music

recording contract   written or spoken agreement between a record company and an artist that sets out their responsibilities, such as creating several albums in a particular number of years

resonate   bring to mind memories and feelings

stereo   system for playing recorded music

subway   underground railway system providing public transportation in a city

venture   new business idea or proposal

Find Out More

Books

Barnes, Geoffrey. *Jay-Z* (Hip Hop). Broomall, Pa.: Mason Crest Publishers, 2007.

Gunderson, Jessica. *Jay-Z: Hip-Hop Icon* (Graphic Library). Mankato, Minn.: Capstone, 2012.

Hasan, Heather. *How to Produce, Release, and Market Your Music* (Garage Bands). New York: Rosen, 2011.

Heos, Bridget. *Jay-Z* (Library of Hip-Hop Biographies). New York: Rosen, 2009.

Lobb, Nancy. *16 Extraordinary American Entrepreneurs*. Portland, Maine: J Weston Walch, 2008.

Nacerous, Roman P. *Jay-Z* (Hip-Hop Headliners). New York: Gareth Stevens, 2011.

Websites

archive.sba.gov/teens/

If you're an aspiring young entrepreneur, check out this "Teen Business Link" website of the U.S. Small Business Administration to get some tips and ideas.

www.pbs.org/independentlens/hiphop/timeline.htm

View a timeline of hip-hop history on this PBS website.

www.themint.org/kids/entrepreneur-challenge.html

If you think you might be interested in starting your own business, take the "Entrepreneur Challenge" at this website. Maybe you could be a titan of business someday!

Music

All Jay-Z records have parental advisory messages because the tracks feature slang and inappropriate words for children. However, one album is more suitable for children than the others—but check with your parent or guardian to make sure it is OK to give it a listen!

Jay-Z: Unplugged. Roc-A-Fella (Def Jam), 2001.

Topics to research

After reading this book, what do you find most interesting about Jay-Z? What business ideas does reading about his success inspire in you? To learn more, you might want to research the following topics:

• Entrepreneurship for young people
• What does a music producer do?
• Def Jam
• Brands

You can visit your local library to learn more about any of these fascinating subjects.

Index